How To Psychoanalyze Someone

How To Make Someone Obsessed With You., Volume 2

Scarlett Kennedy

Published by Scarlett Kennedy, 2018.

While every precaution has been taken in the preparation of this book, the publisher assumes no responsibility for errors or omissions, or for damages resulting from the use of the information contained herein.

HOW TO PSYCHOANALYZE SOMEONE

First edition. October 8, 2018.

Copyright © 2018 Scarlett Kennedy.

ISBN: 978-1386190622

Written by Scarlett Kennedy.

How to Psychoanalyze Someone
Scarlett Kennedy

Copyright © 2018 by Scarlett Kennedy. All Right Reserved.

No part of this publication may be reproduced, distributed, or transmitted in any form or by any means, including photocopying, recording, or other electronic or mechanical methods, or by any information storage and retrieval system without the prior written permission of the publisher, except in the case of very brief quotations embodied in critical reviews and certain other noncommercial uses permitted by copyright law.

Liability disclaimer

The information provided within this Book is for general informational purposes only. While we try to keep the information up-to-date and correct, there are no representations or warranties, express or implied, about the completeness, accuracy, reliability, suitability or availability with respect to the information, products, services, or related graphics contained in this eBook for any purpose. Any use of this information is at your own risk.

The methods describe within this Book are the author's personal thoughts. They are not intended to be a definitive set of instructions for this project. You may discover there are other methods and materials to accomplish the same end result.

The information contained within this Book is strictly for educational purposes. If you wish to apply ideas contained in this Book, you are taking full responsibility for your actions.

The author has made every effort to ensure the accuracy of the information within this book was correct at time of publication. The author does not assume and hereby disclaims any liability to any party for any loss, damage, or disruption caused by errors or omissions, whether such errors or omissions result from accident, negligence, or any other cause.

Introduction

"Well, what do you think it means when they do that?"
"Gee, *why* do they act this way?"
"Does this mean they don't care?"
"Do you think he's acting that way because he's insecure?"

Once upon a time, I was that person. Asking this question, calling my friends at 3 a.m hoping they'd have any logical answer for me. Zero answers were provided. Nothing made sense. Wondering why in the world people behaved the way they did. Slowly losing my mind attempting to understand people - is what motivated me to discover how to analyze any individual's mind.

Seven years ago, I started this journey. Leading people on, dangling their desires in front of their faces, instilling misery, and obsession. Reflecting upon my former motivations for such actions - escapes me now - considering the changes in my values, personality and current life. These rapid changes caused several identity and existential crises.

It's been two years since I've written and published my first book. Since having experienced severe crises, my intent was to delete this entire book, and throw the manuscript in the trash. However, there was a lingering frustration that caused me to complete writing this book. The irritation was hearing people asking this question. Furthermore; the pain, confusion, and loss of sleep these people experienced.

What is psychoanalysis, and why is it important?
PSYCHOANALYSIS IS MAKING the unconscious conscious. Psychoanalysis and therapy is normally associated with excruciating mental

breakdowns on a comfortable couch as they uncover the "dirty" contents of their subconscious minds.

In this case, you are not having a therapy session to uncover your target's scars in order to heal. You're to uncover their scars, lost dreams, untapped potential, their darkest shadows of their unconscious mind to control them - to make them obsessed with you.

Our unconscious mind is in charge of our behavior. The unconscious mind is 90 percent in charge, while our conscious self is 10 percent of our behavior. Only these things reside in the subconscious mind of your target. If you've read my first book - you should know by now that you must identify someone's ideal lover list. The first book was somewhat of an overview. Here, we explore psychoanalysis in depth.

Why I wrote this book

MY READERS WANTED A more concentrated method of psychoanalysis. During my active manipulative bitch years, there were specific things I looked for, to uncover information about a person. All the information I held was powerful. My readers knew this, and asked for it. The way I see it, is our behaviors are something of a metaphor. Psychoanalyzing someone is like someone during the winter season. They are layered in many clothes. Psychoanalyzing is stripping someone of all their clothes, seeing their full vulnerable naked body, and into the abyss of their soul. Internalizing the psychological make up of someone is quite risky. What you do with the information can nurture their hearts with love, or burn their souls. Perhaps both? That's up to you to decide.

Who is this book for?

FOR THOSE OF YOU GOOD souls, you can use this to strengthen your understanding of your partner's needs. Thus, you are able to fulfill their needs and you're able to understand your own needs. If your intentions are not altruistic - you can use this book for your own personal gain. Whether it be getting that girl who otherwise would have never fallen in love with you - to do exactly that. Perhaps you want to stand out in the workplace and climb your way to the top. This will help you curb the time it would have originally taken - without this book.

How is this book different?

A REPETITIVE PATTERN in: books, videos, and other informational products have done their research. Excellent - but have you applied? Application here isn't testing these theories in a lab, or controlled environment. I'm talking psychoanalyzing yourself, taking the theories and applying them to the right people. What I've noticed is people recite studies professionals have done in a lab. While I have much appreciation for the people who conduct the research, followed by the eager people who share the research - that's not going to prove it works on the streets. What's different about me? I've applied all techniques to myself as well as understanding my former targets. Other experts discuss one technique applied to all, that is simply impossible. I cannot stress this enough: one size does not fit all. That's implying you have identical tastes and preferences compared to everyone around you.

How to read this book

I DON'T BELIEVE IN babbling, beating around the bush, or vague explanations. However, I do believe in clarity. Thus, each chapter starts with an introduction, then splits into sub-sections. Each subsection starts off with its own introduction. Followed by: Why it's important, how to discover specific information, an example and lastly, what to do with this information - which serves as the conclusion. No frantically searching for information, no confusion.

Chapter One

Getting Them To Open Up

What's a psychoanalysis without your target opening up?

Why is this important?

YOU NEED REASSURANCE that your victim can feel unguarded around you. Getting your target to open up is allowing them to be vulnerable. Vulnerability shows your target feels safe. Granted, the feeling of safety and security leads to exposure of how they're feeling, and their secrets. Additionally, if they can't tell you anything - you'd only be able to go by behaviours, reactions, and body language. These things are very telling, yet the cherry on top is them - verbally sharing. Sharing dark secrets, and opening up gives anyone the illusion of a bond forming, and growing.

Do you hear people complaining about how other people wouldn't/don't open up to them? There's a reason for that. Here's a comparison of the characteristics of people your target may open up to, versus the types of people your target may close up to.

THE CHARACTERISTICS *of people other people open up to:*

Firstly, to read my book - it requires you to open your mind. If you read my first book: How to Make Someone Obsessed with You, you'll realize you have to open up to listen. Additionally, an open mind is required to play various roles for your target.

People will unconsciously pick up cues that indicate you'd be a great person to vent to or not. If you are sarcastic, narrow minded, and judgemental then why would anyone want to express themselves to you? An open minded person shows they are open to suggestion, and have flexibility on their beliefs. As a result they try to understand the other person's perspective. Here is the list:

HOW TO PSYCHOANALYZE SOMEONE 9

A GREAT LISTENER:

There are four types of listening:

1. Goes in one ear and out the other.

2. You're hearing what they say but you're mentally creating clever responses.

3. You're hearing what they say but your mind is filled with something else; what's for dinner tonight, god look at that pimple, god he's so hot. Oh maybe I should watch that movie tonight.

4. This one is true listening: your mind is clear. You're outright present and only listening to the other person. You're not just listening - you're internalizing what the other person is saying.

Again, people will habitually recognize which listener category you fall into. This'll determine whether someone will open up to you or not.

They trust you:

Trust is the key factor. This is the first thing you'll have to establish. If you can't establish trust, you can't create anything. Without this in mind - the only thing you'll create would be rejection. Trust isn't exclusively about "not telling anyone". Trust is about trusting the person won't judge you. Furthermore they won't put you down. Nor will the person use the confidential information as blackmail further into the relationship.

All these gestures sends the other person a message: you matter. I care about you. Haven't you felt that way around someone who you could be genuine around? That anything you say matters - that you're significant? I know I have. If someone chooses to express themselves to you - don't pride yourself on how great it was. Under those circumstances, don't assume they'll do it again. This is presumptuous. Your target may have been desperate and unknowingly opened up their mouths. Just allow them to do so without perpetually speaking of "that one time they opened to you." Otherwise - it will be one time. Go with the flow. Don't force things. You'll build more rapport.

The ideal candidate for people to NOT open up:

- Judge mental:

A judgemental person doesn't have to say "oh my god, you shouldn't have done that" - to be judgemental. Technically, a judgement is placing a label on something. Thus if you tell someone "that is good." can be great - yet if your target doesn't perceive what they are sharing with you to be good, there will be tension. Given this, the both of you will have different perceptions of what is "good and bad". This can result in your target feeling tense around you. Because they know they wouldn't measure up to your standards of good versus bad. The reason we're judgemental is because that's how we make sense of things in this crazy world. It's how we go from disorder to order.

- Interrupt while you are speaking:

This one is evident. If you can't let someone complete their sentence, put this book down and go learn some manners. Coming back is optional.

- Tell you your feelings aren't valid:

Someone may speak of the past and you'd hear "get it over it, it's the past." Guess what? The past heavily affects us and shapes our perspective. Saying this, invalidates how they're feeling. We are aware this is the past, yet it still affects us. The difference between the people everyone opens up to and the ones people avoid, is the open person will listen and tell you everything is okay.

- Telling people:

Sometimes these types can be hard to spot. An easy indicator of someone like this would be:
"Don't worry I won't tell. Just tell me."
They will tell you other people's secrets.

- Tell the other person how they should and shouldn't feel:

This goes hand in hand with invalidating someone's feelings.

- Fake sympathy:

April 07, 2013 was the day my former best friend committed suicide. A girl called me and "cried." Most people can see through bullshit (unless they're doing the bullshitting.) And, faking sympathy can put you in anyone's bad books. That girl is definitely in my bad books. Plus, you don't have to cry to show me your sympathy!

- They make it a competition:

Whose pain is worse. Who went through worse. The other person makes it about them.
An example:

> I used to have a friend who I would vent to. Then he would start talking about himself. Once, I was venting about my mom then he said "well you're lucky your mom only did that to you - my mom did ____ to me. That's worse. So why do you even feel bad?" This is a person I knew I could never open up to again (although we stayed friends for a few years).

- Person bragging about how many people open up to them:

This is like trophy wives/husbands except they're trophy openers. So really - it's not about caring that you need to open up - it's about playing the rescuer and using this as a trophy. Whoever opens up to this type of person - they've just won another trophy.

That sums up the kinds of people that people wouldn't and shouldn't open up to.

Just notice - do people actually open up to you? Have they said why? Was it a one time thing or was it consistent?

What to do with this information:
IF YOU SERIOUSLY WANT to be able to psychoanalyze your victim you must portray the character of a fantastic listener, and the therapist.

Chapter Two

Body Language

BODY LANGUAGE IS THE language of which our subconscious minds unfold via our body movements, facial expressions, and gestures.

You know the quote actions speak louder than words? Well that's what our bodies do. Our words are only 10% of our minds. Body language showcases 90% of what we truly feel. You can determine if your victim is lying, feeling self assured, troubled, somber, cheerful, among others. Don't listen to their words. Rather, observe their body language.

Body language is essential in communication and psychoanalysis. For psychoanalysis in relation to obsession, body language will determine a few things:

- The truth versus lies.
- What is/has hurt them.
- Attraction versus repulsion.
- What makes them happy, and what their values are.

If they are telling you the truth, or they are lying:

It is in our genes to lie. We sometimes (or always) lie because the truth hurts, lies can be a form of denial, to make our lives appear much more grand than it is. Other reasons for lying can prevent someone from getting hurt, or the complete opposite: to hurt someone. There are a million reasons why we lie. The trick is to figure out when your victim is lying, and how their bodies react when they're lying.

Truthful Body Language:

- Palms facing out.
- Consistent eye contact.
- Steady breath.

Deceptive Body Language:

- Overcompensation.
- Constantly looking around.

- Looking up to the left (for right handers) vice versa, for left handers.
- Blushing.
- Pauses.

If they are attracted to you or repulsed:

One of the utmost critical things in leading someone into their obsession with you, would be attraction. Hate and/or repulsion can make one obsessed as well, but that's not the goal here. A *pleasant* obsession is what we're aiming for, here.

Attractive Body Language:

- Feet pointed towards you.
- Torso pointed towards you.
- Dilated pupils. (If they're constricted - they may be nervous).
- Raised eyebrow.
- Parted lips. (Think primal).
- Upward curve on mouth.
- They look at you when they laugh.
- Smile with their eyes.
- Chest is open, open body language.
- Mirroring your body language.

Repulsed Body Language:

- Feet pointed towards door.
- Torso pointed elsewhere - primarily towards the door.
- Arms crossed - closed body language.
- Forced smiles. (In other words, not smiling with their eyes).
- One word answers.

What has/is hurting them:

Discover what has and currently is hurting them, and you can use this to your advantage. If you've noticed people who return to their lovers who mentally destroy them, it's because the person hurting them has touched a wound. If you've read the first book, you may remember the section about pouring alcohol on their wounds, then soothing their wounds. We do this when making someone obsessed with us, because we are wired to seek out things, friends, partners and circumstances that reflect our deepest emotional wounds until the wounds are healed. However, most people aren't even aware that most if not all, of their actions are based on reflecting this wound. Leverage your victim's lack of awareness, and discover what injuries them through their body language.

Sad and disappointed body language:

- Head bowed down.
- Closed body language.
- Frown - mouth turned down.
- Back, hunched.
- Shoulders forward.

Angry body language:

- Glare
- Furrowed eyebrows.
- Tightened lips/mouth.
- Tightened muscles.

What makes them happy/what their values are:

Provoking someone's deepest wounds is just one of the very few things to make someone obsessed with you. Getting along is something that's very valuable, especially if you plan on having them stick around for a long period. How do you do this? Have similar values. Not having identical values, would mean a lack of happiness which is what we're driven to seek. How do you ascertain your victim's values? An exercise was given to us when I attended *life coaching* college. The name of the game escapes my mind, but we'll call it: The Hell Game. Imagine you reside in hell. Hell is a place that you would without a doubt - loathe. The government has created rules that would make hell, hell. Jot down the *rules* that would make hell, hell.

Here was my list:

- You were prohibited to speak.
- No flossing, showers.
- No learning.

Everyone in the class had different answers. The purpose of the game was to detect what your values are. Sounds simple, maybe even a little childish but I'll explain the exercise to you. Many people become depressed when they can't live by their values. Hell represented what not living by your values meant. The items on the list represent a deeper meaning: what you truly value. Being prohibited to speak means I value self expression, especially verbally. No flossing, and showers means I value personal hygiene. The last one I placed on the list would is evident: I value learning and the acquisition of knowledge.

Now, you're not going to sit down with your target, place a piece of paper and do this exercise with them. That would be dubious to say the least, unless you have that relationship with them. Otherwise, do this exercise without them realizing. Inspect what angers them, what truly breaks their heart. Observing their body language would aid in gaining a clear comprehension of what their values are. Particularly happy body language, but also refer to sad, and angry body language above.

Happy body language:

- Generally relaxed, shoulders back. Muscles relaxed.
- Calm voice.
- Movement fluid.

Not only does body language hold value to conceiving what makes them happy, whether or not they are lying and what makes them feel sorrow, but it can also assist in further unearthing some of the other sections in this book such as defense mechanisms, partners in past lovers and the like.

Chapter Three

Their Past

IT IS RARE PEOPLE SEE the world for what it is. Essentially we are walking filters; projecting our past experiences onto our present experience. People easily manipulated are unaware of the workings of their minds, ignorant of their destructive search for the past to repeat itself again. Take control of your victim by replaying the past they continue to search for. Within this chapter are the major factors that determine how you replay your target's past.

Transport Your Target to Childhood

READERS ASK ME WHAT inspired the beginning of my books. The simple answer would be my crooked family. The parental techniques were built on a strict foundation of power dynamics. At a young age, using my sexuality to obtain my heart's desires, and exploiting men was encouraged - if not the norm. Their parenting techniques primed me to seek out power. Using my desires for good, came the creation of this book.

Why is this important?

OUR RELATIONSHIPS WITH our parents shaped and molded our perceptions - which become our reality. When we were born, we were a blank canvas. The painters of our empty canvas were our parents and/or guardians. The canvas being your mind, and the parents/guardians using the paint brushes to shape and mold your beliefs and perceptions of the world - including love.

A small number of people are aware of the workings of their families, thus yielding to these passed down beliefs. Most people don't stop to wonder: why do I believe this? Why do I behave this way? This loophole in the ignorant human psyche, is where people like us come in; the manipulators, the highly functioning sociopaths, and power seekers.

There are two factors with regards to how our parents/guardians/family influence our perspectives on love. The first factor is your beliefs. Second; what characteristics you seek in prospective partners. If a child witnesses abuse between their parents - they'll believe that's what love is supposed to be. Correlating the first example with the second one - the person with this belief will seek out a partner who will validate these beliefs. In this case, a partner who may be abusive.

How to find out their relationship with their parents:

THERE ARE SPECIFIC questions you should ask if you want to understand your target's relationship with their parents. Firstly, how and what you ask about their relationship with their parents or guardians depends solely on the kind of relationship you have with them, currently. On the contrary, if you've developed a close relationship - this is your cue to ask anything you'd need to know for your benefit. Listen for specific things like if they are close with their family. Observe any patterns in your conversations about their parents. Most people are comfortable discussing their family relations. If not - you'd have a lead. The more dysfunctional the family is, the easier it is to control your target.

Example:

HERE I'LL DISCUSS TWO perfect examples. Jamie* lacked security in her family. Security was what she desperately wanted. There were many indirect ways I provided security for her. One of the few things was displaying a calm and collected mindset. I was firm about my decisions, and made some suggestions about activities we could do during our meetups - that implied how stable I was. Activities such as going to a cafe, having a healthy dinner, and if the weather permitted it - a walk in the park. These activities were the complete opposite of what her standard friends would do: clubbing, drugs, drinking, and the like. She came to me to provide her deepest need: security.

The second example is a textbook case of a person seeking his parental characteristics in his partner. Ryan* is an attractive young man - and knows it. Getting any girl to be his girlfriend was easy for him. There was a pattern for him, he seemed to attract partners who were party goers, and drug users. These women were somehow tied to his mother. Obtaining drugs, alcohol and free passes to parties. Like the women, Ryan's mother had her own choice of drugs: money and power. The ways these women went after drugs, were the same ways Ryan's mother retrieved money and power.

However, one girl came into the picture that got him to commit. While the other women shared similar traits, this girl shared one trait with his mother no other girl has: this woman ridiculed him, criticized him, made him feel unworthy. They're still together. This is the longest he's ever been with a woman.

Our subconscious minds search for people who inflict pain on our deepest wounds. This is because it thinks it is healing itself by finding more wounds, and it is familiar to us.

What to do with this information:
LISTEN CLOSELY TO HOW they describe their relationship with their parents.

Display their parents or guardian's traits they like, and validate their beliefs on love created by their parents. This is why you see people who lived in abusive households and you wonder why they can't just leave their abusive relationship - after all, it is the most logical solution - right? Try to avoid any parental traits your target despises in their parental figures.

Attachment Styles

What is it?

ATTACHMENTS STYLES are ways we attach ourselves in relationships. These develop during our childhood. Our relationships with our parents and/or guardians create our attachment style. There are four main attachment styles in the world of psychology today.

Why is this important to know:

For obsession to occur, you must make your victim *attached*. How? By uncovering their attachment styles, and appealing to it.

Secure Attachment:

This kind is independent within the relationship, without feeling like they're someone else's other half. They are whole and complete.

How you can tell:

- These people are usually confident.
- They don't hide/mask their emotions unless they have to.
- They're open, and won't back away from anything emotional.
- They're proud, but humble.
- They don't run away from love, but they aren't forcing it either.
- Don't get jealous of other people's success - they cheer for them.
- They don't play mind games. (Like we do).

Usually in manipulation we seek out things that people are missing. Secure people aren't missing much. The key is, (this quote) "when you nag control, emasculate weak men, they will bend to your will. Strong men will push you away." -Evan Mark Catz

This doesn't only apply to men, this is for anyone with a secure attachment style. If they are aware of your games, they will back away. Confident and happier people are much harder to seduce. There's no turning back with this kind of attachment style - they will stand their ground.

Example:

Raquel communicates her needs, and understands them. If something bothers her, she'll share her concerns in an assertive manner. She doesn't play games, and will definitely call you out once she realizes you are playing games. Raquel is real, genuine and expects the best, and only the best. She is confident, but not cold hearted.

How to work with this style:

THERE IS A DIFFERENCE between manipulation and growth. Manipulation keeps someone insecure, so you can control them. Growth helps someone grow past their insecurities, and weaknesses - so they can blossom into the beautiful flowers they are!

Confident people are internally dependent, and will work on turning their insecurities into strengths. If you can find a loophole, an insecurity, a lack, they are unaware of - work with that. The main point is - they are unaware of it. This will give you a mysterious seductive effect on them.

Dismissive Avoidant Attachment:

THIS IS THE COLD PERSON in the relationship. It appears they don't need you. They're cold, and will often disassociate from you - and the entire world.

How you can tell:

- Come off as indifferent.
- SEEM **very** independent.
- Easy to dismiss you.

- Will emotionally shut down.
- Push you away.
- Abandon you.
- May isolate themselves.
- Seem disassociated from the world.

Example:

DISMISSIVE AVOIDANTS often appear cold, but they do care. They have shut down their emotions, and are no longer in touch with them. There was someone I met, who we will call Richard. Richard appeared to have a cold dismissive attitude during our time together. All I had to do was discover the source of his coldness. Just as I had suspected - it was his mother. Simple little sayings such as "you're such a baby - stop your moaning and complaining". "Real men don't act like women." Phrases like these can unconsciously train a child to shut their emotions out. Society has conditioned us to associate feeling and expressing our emotions as "girly" meaning weak.

What happens when a dismissive meets someone who brings down their walls? You will be met with a heavy resistance, and possibly more distance. However, take your time and work their minds. The kind of person who brings down your walls will be able to see past all the personas. Slowly, I worked on allowing him to "open up", and he did.

How to work with this style:

- Don't shove commitment down their throat. They will commit if they feel you will not steal their "freedom" however they define freedom.

- Allow them their space and distance.

- Give off the impression that you are just as "independent" as they are.

- Provoke emotions.

- Commitment phobias are usually about control. Control in this case, is about becoming vulnerable, showing the other party who you truly are past the cold exterior. While dismissive avoidants crave this intimacy, it is a daunting reality for them as well.

Fearful avoidant attachment style

THESE TYPES ARE IN a constant state of fear. They fear being too close or too distant from their partner.

How you can tell:

- They're hot and cold.

- They cling to you when you're distant, they're distant when you want to get closer.

Example:

KARRIE EMBODIED THE perfect example of the fearful avoidant. Karrie was a colleague more than anything else. On less professional occasions, her demeanor was cool. She was introduced to Ivan. Casual dating was what they were doing. Everyone around us could see they were slowly building up to something serious. Her cold demeanor still appeared. However when he got close to her, she backed away. When he got frustrated, and decided to keep his distance - she held on tightly. These are the dynamics of the fearful avoidant.

How to work with this style:

- When they're clingy - be distant.

- When they're distant - let it be. Given this, you can try reverse psychology and do the same thing. Especially if you are clingy, they'll wonder why you aren't being clingy.

- Know their fears. Summon when required.

Patterns Between Their Former Flames

HAVE YOU INTRODUCED your new partner to your friends, and they say the same allegation: "s/he reminds/looks exactly like your ex". There's a reason for this - we have patterns and correlations between the lovers and partners we choose and seek. Oftentimes we are too immersed in our pleasurable feelings to recognize any patterns. Let alone break any destructive patterns within romantic relationships, and create new standards for themselves that will serve them in a positive way.

Why is this important?

IF YOU NOTICE PATTERNS between lovers and partners, they will most likely return to the person who portrays prevalent patterns among former partners. Observing patterns will also provide insight as to what their unmet needs are, suppressed sides, values, and idealized versions are. Along with these reasons, the most prominent lover(s) in their lives - your target will attempt to revive their prominent lovers.

All you'll have to do is find out about their ex lovers, by simply asking them. If they talk about their exes without your questions, even better!

Their responses may either be:

- Refusal to speak about their ex.
- Vague answers.
- Bitter rants about their exes.

Responding with the first two answers may designate:

- Indifference towards ex, and have moved on.
- Considerate about your feelings.
- Feelings of embarrassment and/or shame.
- Want to hide their past from you.
- Better yet, has moved on.

However, if they advance their rants about their past lovers - use this as leverage. Watch for micro facial expressions, a gloss in their eyes, a slight frown on the corner of their mouth, or vice versa - a twinkle in their eye, curve on the corner of their lip, parted lips. Sometimes it helps to have an external circumstance to occur so you have an excuse to ask about their ex. For example, see a movie that concerns two parted lovers.

Notice what they repeatedly mention about their exs, and the themes between them.

Maybe their exes were:

- Emotionally unstable. This could mean your target is a rescuer.

- Their ex's always left first. This could mean your target has issues with abandonment, and find companions that validate this belief.

- Had certain career choices. Perhaps their exes were always teachers. This could mean your target likes authority figures, or feel the need to be "lead" by a teacher.

If they don't talk about their exes - provoke them. Get closer to their friends, have their friends share information unwillingly. Do anything to retrieve information - even if it is bleak.

Example:

I had known someone who we'll call Prince (don't ask about these peculiar nicknames), since I was fifteen. I was his first girlfriend - his first everything. Eventually, we had to break up because he moved eight hours away. Our friendship remained intact. We would talk about our love lives, and there's always a recurring theme between the women he would fall for - including myself. Prior lovers are emotionally unstable. They were one large mess waiting to be cleaned up. He complained about it. However, he would've left if he hated the emotionally unstable women. People are suspended and return if something psychologically serves them - even if it is deemed negative. As soon as I become emotionally stable, and flaunted it - his attraction towards me diminished.

What to do with this information:

RECOGNIZE ANY PREVALENT patterns your target is drawn to, then depict the universal patterns that keeps them coming back for more. Stay away from any patterns that frighten them. If you dare to provoke frightening patterns, make it erotic.

Chapter Four

Their Belief Systems

BELIEF SYSTEMS ARE self fulfilling prophecies. Whatever we believe, is exactly what we search to validate a specific belief. This is important when controlling someone because if you do not validate a belief, they may run from you. Have you noticed people with low self esteem stay with people who validate their unworthiness? On the other hand, if someone is trying to lift them up they don't show any signs of attraction - *at all*. Why is this happening? You can credit the good old trusty belief system for that. With that in mind, this chapter will explore multiple ways to ascertain your target's belief systems in order to infiltrate their minds.

Who are you?

WHO IS YOUR VICTIM?

We all identify with something. Our egos created identities for us to make sense of this world. It is how we create order. This is a vague question. What does it even mean? How does one even answer such a strange and vague question?

No one can know for sure. Yet there is a pattern between the answers people will give you to the question: "Who are you?"

Here they are:

"Oh - I'm Linda's husband!"

"I'm the instructor for this class!"

"I'm the CEO for (insert company name)"

Sure - these are roles we play in society. These are things we do. Nonetheless what does it mean to explain who we are? Again - who knows.

Why is this important?

HOW TO PSYCHOANALYZE SOMEONE 31

IT'S IMPORTANT TO APPREHEND what your target concludes their identity is. It's easier to learn what they identify with if they're constantly placing labels on themselves.

Once you're aware of this you'll need to break down their identity. Question their identity - make them feel unsure of their identity. Just as they feel doubtful, they will begin to rely on you to make them feel psychologically secure again. This is just like any other technique in the first book. Except they are all applied differently. An identity is like a filter. Our identities filter out our reality.

Example:

A MAN I'VE MENTIONED lots of times on my blog - Peter, repeatedly says to me "I don't know why I'm unsatisfied. I'm an engineer for god's sake". You know what this indicates? He bases his self worth on his career. Several people will base their identities on their looks. Other examples include: the car they own, how well they can perform Krav Maga, and their past childhood.

What to do with this information:

WHATEVER IT IS THEY identify with - seize that and break it down. I wouldn't say anything - when Mr. Engineer was hoping I'd praise him. What he expects me to say is: "yes you are a god." with a huge grin on my face. Truth is, I don't care that he is an engineer. Once they start becoming insecure, they will depend on you to make them feel secure. Once you detect they are becoming anxious, this is when you say "so tell me more about your work. I'd love to hear more." The key is bringing them on an emotional roller coaster. One of they key foundations in making someone obsessed with you. (See: Anxious much?)

Their Sexual Fantasies

Sexual fantasies are an extension of fantasies - they satisfy a psychological need. They all emulate our inner selves, and our belief systems. If you take a closer look at someone's personality, you'll notice their sexual fantasies may reflect an aspect of their personality. A person who craves attention may fantasize about gang bangs, someone who is passive will seek submission and domination. Although every now and then, seeing someone's personality at face value - their fetishes will genuinely surprise you. For example, many people have the misconception that a dominant person would be assertive in bed, while in fact s/he may be submissive as hell.

Another topic regarding sex, is countless people believe sex is the end game - once a person has sex with you - they've possessed you.. Right? *Wrong*. Sex can often facilitate someone's obsession with you further. This is because you've shared another part of yourself and it only makes your target feel closer to you.

Why is this important?

Sexual desires are just another way of our minds fulfilling a psychological need. If your relationship isn't platonic, there may be a form of sex or some sort of sexuality.

Common sexual fantasies and potential meanings:
Being walked in on:
Chronic shame, lack of boundaries/privacy in childhood.
Dominant:
Dominant personality. Wants control. Another one could be, they do not have control in their lives.
Falling for married people and/or emotionally unavailable.
Issues with abandonment. If you have issues with abandonment:
You may have these fantasies because if you go for someone who is emotionally unavailable, or married or both.. Then there is no worry about abandonment...because it's a self fulfilling prophecy.

Rape:

It's not so much about rape. It's about pleasure - if a guy or girl breaks into your house just to have sex with you, they'd pretty much do anything to be with you. Again, it's about going all the way. If you have fantasies about doing the raping - get therapy. It's probably about control. You may feel powerless to women or men, and want to take back control... by raping them.

Being slapped around:

Low self esteem - undeserving. There's also a possibility the person with this fantasy had parents who did not provide any healthy boundaries - if at all.

Submission/tied up:

This person may always be tense - thus they have the desire to lose control. This fantasy helps them lose control - even if it isn't physically.

Example:

ONE OF MY TARGETS, Timothy was a child stuck in a man's body. He literally acted like a little child, begging his mother to buy him toys and gadgets most boys would have outgrown by their tenth birthday. His sexual fantasy? A mother in bed. His mother was a typical mother - overbearing yet nurturing. The only thing missing? Discipline. Someone needed to straighten him out - and it would be me. Oftentimes he would push his mother's boundaries to test her limits. She never asserted any boundaries, nor did she know how to. That's where I stepped in. Leading up to the moments we finally had sex, I would allow him to catch me in moments where I would "discipline" people. During a dinner he was attending with some friends, someone called begging for me to save them because they were having a bad drug trip. Keeping the frustration in my voice down, I asked the person on the other line what they "ate." Bursts of giggles ensued as he replied "Why are you so serious?!"

My irritable levels skyrocketed. "Look, if you don't answer my fucking question I'll come over there and have to discipline you." Shocked expressions wavered over me, some avoided looking at me. Timothy? He stared with a glimmer in his eyes. He was the first person to question the identity of the person on the other line. The tone in his voice was filled with a childlike curiosity, while others expressed concern. While a majority of the crowd did not want to admit it - some felt shame. The feeling of shame derived from my lack of self control, my inadequate ability of timing. Couldn't I wait until *after* the dinner to "discipline" the mystery person? No. But it's in progress.

Not only did I not care what the others at dinner thought, I loved that most members at the dinner table felt disturbed by my emotional impulses. At the time, all I cared about was pushing Timothy's buttons - so he could push mine...

The spark in his eye, the excitement of a little boy on Christmas morning he displayed, was enough to pursue the strict mother persona with Timothy. As I observed his mother further, it was evident what his mother lacked was order. Some people yearn to be put in their place. Timothy wondered what it would be like unconsciously.

Finally, the fateful day came. Timothy was misbehaving. After experimenting with the orderly strict motherly role, it became habitual. I loaded my discipline skills and techniques on him, and he glowed. I showed both sweet nurturing and strict mother traits up until we had sex.

What to do with this information:

REPRESENT THE NEEDS emotionally, not just sexually. Sex isn't usually required to someone obsessed with you, as long as you can indirectly fulfill and represent their psychological desires and needs. Sex is just a bonus.

What Kind of Thinker Are They?

THROUGHOUT YOUR STANDARD educational life, the terms "visual, auditory, or kinaesthetic learner" may ring a bell. Studying, teaching and learning through your mind's preferred learner type, will aid in absorbing information further, and the ability to recall the information would not only help a student pass tests and exams, but feel more confident in recall of the information. So what's this got to do with making someone fall in love with you? Awareness of the method your target's mind receives and gives information can help you communicate, and appeal to their self interests much more effectively. It would be as if you are learning their own language.

Visualize this interaction:

GIRLFRIEND: I'VE HEARD some bad news from Megan. We need to talk." (Auditory)

Boyfriend: "I see. What did she tell you?" (Visual)

Gf: "I've heard you've been still talking to your ex." (Auditory)

Bf: "Look, I'm sorry." (Visual)

Gf: "I want to hear why you're still talking with her." (Auditory)

From the looks of this interaction - it is going downhill. It is most likely turning into an argument. The conversation could be much more fluid if each or one partner would have adjusted to both or one representational systems. Here is an example of the boyfriend using his girlfriend's learning style.

Girlfriend: I've heard some bad news from Megan. We need to talk." (Auditory)

Boyfriend: "What did she tell you?"

Gf: "I've heard you've been still talking to your ex." (Auditory)

Bf: "Listen, I'm sorry." (Visual)

Gf: "I want to hear why you're still talking with her." (Auditory)

What to do with this information:
JUST LIKE IN THE MOTIVATION section, it's child's play to motivate your target when you're literally speaking their language - precisely with how their brain perceives information and knowledge.

Insults

"She's fat."
"He's too short."
"They're too stupid.

You've heard all these ridiculous insults before. If "insults" are not verbalized in a constructive manner, don't take it personally. The reason being most insults are a result of projection. After all - misery loves company.

Why this is important:

When the mind can't accept something about ourselves, it tries to pass it onto someone else - like a hot potato. Insults are a byproduct of projection. Insults can give you insight on what the person believes about themselves. We're always projecting our inside world onto the outer world. Insults are just one form of projection. There are many others mentioned in this book. Once you discover what their insecurities are, use it to your advantage.

What to listen for:

LISTEN FOR THINGS THEY criticize you and other people about. It's usually projection when it isn't true. When people criticize others - they unconsciously seek out their own insecurities.

Examples:

SOMEONE WHO HAD ACNE problems will constantly criticize people about their skin. You'll also notice they may stare at your or someone else's skin often. Someone who is hard on themselves about work related things, may call you lazy. Even if it isn't true, they'll find reasons and excuses to call you lazy.

Lastly, insults can come in the form of jokes as a passive aggressive way of insulting you. For example, "you're stupid, I'm kidding!".

One thing to beware of, is you may project. The way you react to someone's sense of humor can indicate your beliefs as well. If a joke hurts you, analyze and heal the insecurity/emotional wound.

What to do with this information:
REMEMBER TO TAKE THEIR insults with a grain of salt, then capitalize their insecurities for your personal gain. You can either rub salt on their insecurities then make them feel better, or use it to feed their egos.

What Motivates Them?

WHY DID I WRITE THIS book? What prompted you to get out of bed on the weekend besides a full bladder? Why are you doing the things you do? Everything starts with a motivation.

Why is this relevant to psychoanalysis?
BEHIND EVERY BEHAVIOUR, action, thought, and desire is a psychological motivation. The primary motivation is to satisfy these needs. When you investigate further into your target's motivations, you can fulfill their needs, thus you become their first motivation. The hunger for you will increase as you uncover what propels them.

How you can tell what motivates them:
LET'S USE EXERCISE as an example. Are they doing working out for aesthetic reasons or for health reasons? E.g. blood circulation.

Examine what they reveal about the topic. Are they always talking about how they're starting to shed some pounds, or are they discussing how warm their feet feel now? It doesn't have to be one reason. It can be both. Usually one reason is more dominant than the other. Learn which one it is. Listen for precise detail.

Another example:
SOMEONE YOU KNOW INGESTS a substantial amount of drugs. Is it because it helps them find meaning? Are they trying to escape from his or her reality? Listen to what they say about their experiences on drugs. And how it made them feel etc.

Note: you can't be presumptuous and create reasons as to why people are doing the things they do. Two people can do something or behave the same way - but do it for two various reasons. One girl may smoke cigarettes because she believes it'll suppress her appetite. While the other girl may smoke because she thinks it's sexy. Therefore, you must watch carefully. You'll notice patterns. Then, you can safely connect it with the reason they are motivated. Power and control is what motivated me to write this book and start my blog.

Motivational words:
PEOPLE HAVE DIFFERENT words that motivate them. The common ones are:
I HAVE to
I WANT to
I NEED to
I DARE you.

Notice what they say about their errands, chores, whatever they call it. You may hear it in your daily conversation.

Here is an example:

You: what are you doing today?
Other person: I HAVE to finish a couple of errands today.
You: what do you HAVE to do?
Other person: I NEED to clean up my car.

They may say other words, but notice the ones they say often. An example of you, using it could be:

You: hey, today we HAVE to go see a movie.

Using their motivational words is speaking their language. It is more likely to motivate your target. Their motivational words are how they perceive motivation. If they have to, it's a chore. They are obligated. If they use the word want, it's more of a desire.

What to do with this information:
IN ADDITION TO USING their motivation words, represent what motivates them. If social status drives them - represent what social status means to them.

What's So Funny?

"DO YOU WANT TO HEAR a funny joke?" your date inquires as the two of you sit down at your table.

You give an unsound smile "yes."

"Why did the skeleton have no date to the party?"

You blink your eyes, confused and wonder where the *funny joke* is? Laughter in the background occurs as your date answers "because they had *no body* to go with." All you want to do is cringe more than laugh, but you express a giggle anyway.

Relatable? That's because it is. This example is more exaggerated, but I've been on both ends. And hey, I find bad jokes hilarious. We've all met, and will meet people who do not share similar comedic tastes. If you've ever wondered why some people find something funny, while others don't, the answer lies within someone's belief system.

Why is this important?
SOMEONE'S HUMOUR IS like a freudian slip. Whatever makes someone laugh, resonates with them. When people say "once you make them laugh, you have them." Meaning, they've hit a gold mine. Here, you can discover your victim's deepest buried beliefs.

How to find out:
WATCH A MOVIE THEY believe to be funny (hopefully you do too).
 Observe what makes them laugh hysterically, even observe what they chuckle about.
 Listen to their stupid jokes.
 This will provide insight into who they are. They wouldn't laugh if it wasn't at the back of their minds in the first place, this goes for other reactions you notice. E.g. a somber look on their face, anger, etc.

Examples:
A VICTIM OF MINE WOULD prefer to sit at his house and watch movies all day. Each time something demeaning came on about a woman, he would laugh at it. Not chuckle - he laughed his fucking ass off. Knowing this, connecting all the dots in his personality - he has no respect for women. The manner in which he spoke to me confirmed his sense of humor. He would "jokingly" call me a slut, said I looked like a whore when I wore x,y and z.

What to do with this information:
YOU CAN USE THIS INFORMATION to appeal and understand your target better. Whatever you chose to do - is ultimately your choice.

Chapter Five

Defense Mechanisms

UNLESS YOU'RE AN EMOTIONAL masochist or drama queen, you tend to steer clear of any pain. Our minds have little to no tolerance to any pain, therefore creates defense mechanisms to protect itself. At face value, you may find yourself irritated by your target's behaviour. Perhaps they go cold. Maybe they start blaming others for something going south. The answer lies in someone's defense mechanisms.

Defense Mechanisms

EVERYONE COPES DIFFERENTLY. Have you ever looked at someone, and wondered why they coped the way do? Why are they reacting this way? Why are you reacting this way? This is simply your psychological defense mechanisms.

Why do we have them/why is this important?
IT IS OUR MIND'S WAY of protecting, and defending ourselves, from traumatic events, and strong emotions.

Note: there are many other psychological defence mechanisms, however I've only listed the common ones that are important to work with, to make someone obsessed with you.

Compartmentalization:
THIS IS LIKE DISASSOCIATION. Except, you don't completely disassociate. Only parts of yourself are disassociated.
How you can tell:
If they appear distant from different parts of their lives, they are compartmentalizing.
Example:

A woman who is cheating on her husband may disassociate. But with work - she isn't, because she loves her job.

How to deal:
Whatever they are compartmentalizing, know that they may be unsatisfied. This is your chance to fill in the unsatisfactory gaps in their lives.

Disassociation:
DISASSOCIATION IS WHEN someone removes themselves from reality, by distancing themselves from reality. Instead of a subjective reality, it becomes objective.

How you can tell:
They seem bored, cold and distant all the time.

Example:
Dan, is someone who is always disassociated. He was always talking about his fantasy world. A world filled with poetry, and rock music. When I got two tickets to a Slash concert (from guns and roses) I knew exactly whom to call; Dan. When he dissociates himself he goes into a fantasy world. I brought this fantasy to life. With the concert in mind, he finally got to live out the fantasy he yearned for, and associated me, as the enabler. As the person who isn't trying to "ground them." Or the person to "bring them back to reality." Rather, the person who takes him away from it.

How to deal:
Take it further, and be their escape. Rather than bringing them back to reality, bring them into an exotic fantasy world. Disassociation is essentially removing one's self from reality. So take advantage of this. It can be in the form of the things the two of you do, or a journey/adventure the two of you go on. It's about their experience with you.

Fantasies:

(SEE: WHAT'S YOUR TARGET's deepest fantasy?)

Acting out:

ACTING OUT IS WHEN someone expresses their emotions in extreme and/or childish ways.

How to tell:

This one is very obvious. They'll start yelling, screaming, throwing material. Whatever floats their boat.

Example:

Ryan was one of the coolest guys I'd ever met. I always looked at him and wondered if his cool attitude was a way to cover up any undisclosed rage he had. While I bottled up my emotions well, my voice devoid of any emotions and everything about my demeanor screamed ice queen - I told him I secretly wanted to walk out on the streets and start fights with random people. He smirked and agreed he shared the same fantasy. To fast forward, one day he called me. He needed to vent. Backstabbing friends betrayed him, and it hurt. We were on the phone for about twenty minutes, and I asked "why don't we meet, perhaps we can both detox our frustrations?" He asked what happened what my issues were and I told him I'd explain when we met. When we met, I explained to him I was furious and now was a good time to act on my wildest impulses. He opened his mouth slightly to disagree and inject a pinch of moral dose in my veins. But, he didn't. He stared at me with a morbid curiosity, before answering "same here - but first, tell me what happened?"

My frustrations were based on recurring problems with my psychopathic family. Expressing my anger, I felt my blood boiling at the highest temperature possible. The volume in my voice grew louder, and more aggressive as I shared what caused me to be in this current state. I took a deep breath and explored the vicinity with my eyes. I spotted a bar and asked if I could continue my rant while we had a few shots.

As the shots began to pour, so did my rage. I had my eye out on the stereotypical misogynist at the bar. My angry drunken felt it would be satisfying to fight a misogynistic man rather than another drunk angry woman. Triggering him was the first thing I knew I had to do. First, I stared at him. When I captured his attention - I blatantly flirted with the man sitting next to him. He nudged his friend and whispered something. To this day, I do not what was within that whisper. I also nudged Ryan and told him that muscular misogynist type guy across the bar was who I wanted to fight. He agreed he also wanted to fight him. The layout of the bar was that when Ryan and I, had to leave, we had to walk past woman hater and his woman hater friend. Ryan placed his arm around me as we walked past them and they watched. Given this, Ryan unbelievably walked straight to his face and asked why these creeps were staring at my ass. They weren't - it was a coy to start a fight. It worked.

At the end of it all, Ryan treated me like his favorite drug of choice. He knew I was bad for him. Yet, he continued to come back for more anyway. The day he overdosed on me was the day he finally lost a physical fight. He sought them out the way addicts looked for their vices. He needed them. One day, his family noticed a pattern. I was *always* there when he placed himself into dangerous altercations. The last day I ever saw Ryan was when they questioned why I never stopped it. While I denied it, I wondered how they knew that. That was when his brother shot me a foul look, and interrupted. "The last time I tried to stop it - you stood there smiling like a psycho."

At the end of the night, I was kicked out and forbidden to see him. Ryan's parents threatened to kick him out, and that's the last thing he wanted. All he wanted was to throw his fists onto someone's face, have a few trophy bruises, go home and have a good night's rest. But, without my encouragement - he was lost.

How to deal:

Allow them to act out. Parts of ourselves want to act out with people we feel it is safe to do so, with. Someone who won't judge them. Be the enabler. Be the person they feel safe to act out with. As long no one is hurt in any shape, or form. It's beneficial for one's mind and soul. Our deeper selves want to let go of our social restrictions, and act out without any restrictions. To be as crazy, rude, and rowdy as we can be.

Sublimation:
(See: why they chose their career?)

Projection/transference:
WHEN YOU PROJECT YOUR inner beliefs, desires, what an ideal, person, or world would be like, emotional wounds onto someone.
How to tell:
If someone starts going on about how you should be doing something a certain way, or be a certain way. They are projecting. They are also projecting if they start assuming things about you - that you didn't tell them. This is because our imagination fills in missing pieces of information about you, or anything.
Example:
I went on a trip to New York City, with a girlfriend of mine: Sarah. Sarah and I wanted to treat ourselves to a beautiful gourmet meal, so we had dinner in the most luxurious restaurant in town. There was a man sitting across from me, and he stared at me the entire time. I wondered if he even blinked. I wanted to test him to see if he would talk to me. So I got up, and told Sarah I was going to the restroom. His table was along the way. Before I knew it I heard:

"Excuse me, miss." In a heavy German accent.

"Yes?" I asked innocently.

"I was wondering if I could buy you a drink? Get to know you better?"

I snickered, and walked away.

As I got back to my table, there was a drink waiting for me. Sarah was mocking the

German man's voice. "The drink is for you my beautiful dear."

As the night went on, I realized the German man wasn't so disappointing, after all. I gave him my number, and he started chatting me up.

All of a sudden, he goes on to say:

"Having sex for the first time would be magical for you."

I giggled. "Now, please tell me what you're talking about."

"I've been hurt before, so I figured if I could be with a virgin, she wouldn't hurt me."

I was confused, but realized what was going on. The man thought I was a virgin. ***But, why?***

He was projecting onto me:

- His ideals, (a virgin, who won't leave an emotional scar.)
- Hurts (girls have hurt him in the past.)
- My innocent look triggered his imagination to project onto me.

Projection starts when there is a trigger. For the German man, it was my innocent face.

How to deal:

Allow them to project onto you. If it's an obsessive, ideal projection, project it back. Project it back by representing whatever it is they are projecting onto you. Remember you can NEVER directly mention you are representing what they are projecting.

Compensation:

IF SOMEONE IS LACKING/feeling insecure about a compartment in their lives, they compensate in another area of their lives.

HOW TO TELL/EXAMPLES:

- They'll overcompensate. For example, Mr. Griffin showed he had nothing to offer but money. He didn't even have that much money either. He made $200,000 annually. Big deal. He would always say, obnoxiously, "I'm an engineer." When someone would make him feel stupid.

- They'll compare. For example, when I was younger I had a family relative who always talked about people aging. She'd say "oh my god. That woman is aging so badly." "Thank god, I'm still skinny." Truth is, she was aging. We all are. I could see it, although I kept my mouth shut. She knew deep down inside she was aging. It showed. She used her weight as compensation.

How to deal:
Figure out what they may be compensating for. Then fill in that lack. For example, someone who believes they are lacking in the beauty department, will compensate by having an abundance of wealth. Filling in that lack would be making them feel beautiful.

Rationalization:
REFRAMING SOMETHING into a different light, or creating a different explanation for what and why something has occurred.

EXAMPLE/HOW TO TELL:
Mary, a narcissistic "friend" of mine, had a long time boyfriend break up with her. His reason was that he didn't appreciate that she needed to depend on him financially, and she was in her forties. Her rationalization was "I was too good for him, he felt intimidated, and he couldn't ever live up to me. So he ended it."

How to deal:
Nod your head, smile, and look pretty.

Denial:
WHEN SOMEONE REFUSES to accept the truth, reality, and facts.
How you can tell:
(See: what are they NOT)
Example:
Mr. Griffin was my next door neighbor. He was unhappy in his marriage, he was in denial about it. He would constantly say "my wife is great." "I love her." He would find every excuse not to go home to see her face. Little slips and passive aggressive comments about her, would rise to the surface. I saw how in denial he was - about her. I decided to seize the opportunity, to be the distraction he was looking for. His words said he was in love and happy. His actions showed me, he despised his wife. (See: what are they NOT?)

His actions showed he tried to find every excuse in the book to get away. He would mask them by "wanting to take me out to show me a good time." Every time she was home, he had "a meeting." (With me.) When she wasn't home, he was relaxed and happy. I knew he was the rescuer type, so I played the damsel in distress and got him to drive me to school, drive me to work. I turned him into my personal chauffeur...

That is, until his wife found out. She wanted a divorce because she suspected we were having sex. Which was not the case. He just wanted a distraction.

His reaction? Take a wild guess.
How to deal:
Allow them to be in denial. You'll see what they're in denial about, and be the distraction from what they're in denial about.

Why They Chose Their Career Path?

HOW TO PSYCHOANALYZE SOMEONE 53

OUR VOCATIONS ARE WHAT takes up most of our time, minds, and days. Most of our identities emanate from what we do, careers avail us survive in this world through this currency of engendering more social circles, and primarily: money. Why did your target cull their career path? One of the answers lies in sublimation. Sublimation is a psychological defence mechanism where our repressed and/or suppressed adverse aspirations are transferred onto socially acceptable activities, desires, careers, habits.

Why is sublimation important?
SUBLIMATION IS EXCLUSIVELY true for people who play the noble character within society, yet they are mostly drawn to people who candidly express their base selves. Noble knight in shining armors and modern mother Teresa's' tend to be drawn to bad boys/girls because sublimation stimulates their suppressed/repressed desires to be bad, wrong, immoral or destructive.

How to find out why they chose their career path:
SIMPLY ASK THEM. CORRELATE what their reasons are versus their actions. Are they connected or severely contrasting each other? A perfect thing to listen for would be stories they share about work, coworkers, and what events leading up to and inspiring the decision to pick their career. If they have a job where they had no choice, ask them what they would've chosen given they *had* the choice.

Let's use the cop as an example. You inquire why he chose to be a cop, and he answers he wants to serve and protect. Yet, he perpetually discusses murder, and *stupid* people he's arrested that day. You see the sublimation here?

Examples:

A COP I DATED CHOSE that career path because of control and power. He explained it was for justice. However, when deciphering his actions - it was not for the people who lived in the community - it was justice for himself. A career as a police officer was his way of getting his own justice, and revenge because he's been bullied in the past.

Someone who has the desire for power may become a business person. Yet this is a different power compared to power the cop wanted. Cop wants to exert physical force over his bully and people who remind him of his former bullies. Rich boy wanted to exercise his power by having money because growing up poor made him feel powerless.

What to do with this information:

ULTIMATELY, SUBLIMATION suppresses and/or represses one's unfavourable selves. Take advantage of people's sublimation by provoking their suppressed and hidden sides.

What are they *not*?

I mentioned one thing that reveal people's true colours, is what they endeavor to project themselves as. Another more vigorous thing is the antithesis - what they perpetually verbalize they *AREN'T*.

Why is this important?

- This important because it shows they're in denial about.

- What they're trying so desperately trying to cover up.

- They may feel shame about it - but want to potentially explore.

- Society has made them feel shame about feeling and/or thinking this way.

- For example: An overly sadistic person may seem overly nice because they're trying to cover up their sadistic views. (I'm guilty of this.)

Example 1:

One guy that I had known, we'll call him Peter. He continued disclosing "I'm not trying to control you." - but he was. The reason being no person isn't going to continuously say that, unless they are that way. He was unconsciously trying to cover up his tracks. In essence, who are you trying to convince, you or me?

Example 2:

One of my friends always expressed "I'm NOT codependent" on anyone. She may not have been codependent, but it was her mind's way of aspiring to forfend herself from genuinely becoming that way. It showed in her comportment every time she needed avail, or got proximate to someone, she'd become defensive and reluct any avail or any intimacy with anyone. Because she had the belief she wouldn't be independent anymore. She'd have to be "codependent."

Now, we have two reasons, for why people are endeavoring to convince us what they're NOT:

1) This is their authentic nature, but their subconscious mind doesn't want to welcome it. Consequently, their minds handle it by perpetually telling other people what they aren't.

2) Their subconscious mind doesn't want them to be this way, and is trying to prevent (what they're not) from becoming the truth.

How to take advantage of this:

You have to attest if they're expressing x,y,z because they are that way, or they're undertaking not to become this way. You can decipher this, by canvassing their actions - especially what they're resistant to.

Example:

Let's use Peter as an example as someone who is this way and trying to cover it up. I kenned he was endeavoring to control me, because every time I told him I would go out, he would ask me "Who are you going out with?" "Why are you guys going out?"

"What are you guys going to do?" He would dissimulate it as "Well, I just want to know. I hope you have fun!"

Genuinely, once I connected the dots - he was controlling. What gave it away was, he always had to ken if I was going out with a female or male.

One day, I was going out to meet with a guy and he went abaft my back to a mutual friend,

verbalizing "why is she always going out with different guys?" Affirmative, he's jealous. Yes, he's controlling. The more weird, crazy out of control things, the more he wanted and tried to control me. Hysterical thing was, he was espoused. We weren't even dating either. We were coworkers. This is an example of someone who is what they claim they're not.

HOW TO PSYCHOANALYZE SOMEONE

If they are trying not to be this way:
YOUR TARGET WILL COMMENCE slipping, then they'll become conscious of their behaviour - and snap out of it. Followed by extreme demeanors that will overcompensate for their sides they are trepidacious of, and do not want to become.

Example:
AN ALTRUISTIC GUY WHO endeavors to suppress his naughtiness, may react positively to something deplorable/naughty, then retort back to his spineless side. In high school there was Juan. He was incredibly nice, and saccharine. We went to the mall, and I provided explicit details about when I made out with my friend Michelle. He was getting a erection, and he kept persisting for more information, then immediately returned to his altruistic persona - once he realized how he was exposing himself. Leaks of his sexuality were emerging, however he covered up his boner, and sexuality with his backpack and shame was what gave it away.

What do with this information:
SANCTION THESE REPRESSED/and/or suppressed sides to gradually emerge. It genuinely wants to materialize. Maybe they have a sadistic streak. Maybe they are trying to be more masculine by covering up that they have the desire to become much more feminine. Instigate it a minute. Converse about certain topics around it.

For example: if he or she is controlling, discuss doing stuff that they can't control. If a guy is wanting to be more feminine, and postulating you're female - just be more feminine, and this'll sanction him or her to live through you.

There may be some resistance. Resistance is the best thing, because their desire is growing much more vigorous. Your job is to break down that resistance. Once you discern an abundance of resistance, you can pull back, then instigate. Rinse and reiterate.

The Codependent Triangle

Codependent relationships are depicted in the media as the ultimate relationship goal. Relationships are comprised of intense passion. Often times this passion appears to be dangerous. The truth is, the readers of this book and their victims have a codependent streak - which fall into three types: the rescuer, victim, or prosecutor. Toxic loves are often romanticized; relationships like Bonnie and Clyde. This chapter will discuss how to deal with the three types on the codependent triangle, and how to utilize it to your advantage.

What is it?

It is a triangle in the psychology community that shows destructive behaviors and roles in conflicting interactions/arguments.

Why is it important?

Knowing which destructive role you and your target play, can assist how you interact in an argument and the relationship, overall. You can prepare yourself for how the other person may react. Discovering where they fit on the codependent triangle, can make your victim much more dependent on you.

Rescuer:

The rescuer is always trying to save someone. There are two types of rescuers: the ones who are situational: they save you from awful situations. The second type is the moral rescuer: they try to transform you into a good person. (See: the rescuer, in target section of "How to Make Someone Obsessed with You):

How you can tell:

(See: the rescuer, in target section of "How to Make Someone Obsessed with You):

"Let me help."
"We should."
"You should."
"I'm a good person."
"Look at all I do for you."

How to deal:

Tell them you don't need their services right now, and when you do, you'll ask.

When you want to capitalize on the rescuer type - make them rescue you. Before you do, you must understand if they are the situational or moral rescuer. Once you do, you can act accordingly.

Victim:

Someone with a victim mentality believes that they are powerless, helpless, and hopeless to life's circumstances. Some victims do this to get attention or hope to be rescued.

How you can tell:

- They're always talking about the people that are wronging them.
- The universe is mocking them.
- Poor me.
- They're constantly feeling sorry for themselves.
- The worst things always happen to them.
- Talking about their sob stories.
- "I'm helpless."

How to deal:

SAY NO. HAVE LIMITS. Verbalize your boundaries. Then prepare yourself for a guilt trip. Try to discuss solutions instead. Once they notice that you are *in*dependent rather than *co*dependent, they'll depend on you because this will satisfy the lack they have which is independence.

If you want to take advantage of this, place them into a situation where they can feel sorry for themselves, and you're able to give them the attention and sympathy they require for fuel.

Persecutors:

THEY CAN'T ACCEPT RESPONSIBILITY. Putting the blame onto anyone or anything they can, but themselves.

How you can tell:

"It's all your fault."

"It's because of this , because of that."

"I'm right, you're wrong."

"Are you crazy?"

How to deal:

Just sit there and listen. Persecutors receive their fuel from your responses. They expect, and want a response from you. If you don't feed into their persecutions, it'll anger them much more. However, they can't say anymore, if they don't have anymore fuel. (Your response).

Taking advantage of this could either mean you do not give into any of their crap, or give them something to complain or start a fight. Persecutors are most likely to fit into the drama queen victim type. Fulfill their need for drama.

Chapter Six

Emotions

I CONSIDER MOST OF my readers as marketers. They carry similar mindsets; manipulating, using people's own psychology against them, distorting facts to control the consumer. Our emotions have the ability to cloud our judgement, and twist our thoughts into ones that will appeal or amplify the emotion. People usually associate an emotional person as someone who cries often. In fact, being emotional relates to all emotions. The specific definition of emotional just relates to an intense feeling. What human beings are seeking could be an intense feeling of security, vanity, adventure, feeling horny. Given this, there are certain emotions the greatest seducers and seductresses play with: anxiety, uncertainty, lust, curiosity, hope. When we become dependent on something or someone, one of the reasons is because they provide an emotion(s) no other can fulfill. When pleasant emotions are triggered and amplified, we feel alive. Be the only person they can rely on to feel alive.

Anxious Much?

HEIGHTENING YOUR VICTIM's anxiety creates dependence. The first step is

discovering how they behave when they become anxious. That will lead to you

comprehending what makes them anxious, unless they are always anxious. A person who is invariably anxious is easier to control, and influence.

Why is this important?

As I've mentioned earlier, inducing anxiety within your target will create

dependence. Anxiety specifically will create dependence. The reason being:

codependent relationships arise out of fear, and anxiety - not love. (A common misconception.) Society conditioned us to believe fear, and anxiety is what the meaning of love is. In high school my classmates and

I had to recite a play. Many of you know it: Romeo and Juliet. Numerous people claim Romeo's undying love for Juliet was

romantic, and authentic love. Their relationship was not true love. The relationship was desperate and codependent. You may see other people both in your life and onscreen - in codependent relationships. The people are attached by the hip. The couple that are inseparable - even when space is vital.

What do you see? Do you see confidence and security? Or do you see desperation, a lack of personal power and control? A wild need to tighten their clench due to the fear of abandonment? I guarantee you see the latter. The precise reason you must instigate anxiety within your target.

Why do people become anxious?

MANY PEOPLE DISREGARD their emotions. What these people don't understand is the reason we have emotions. Our "negative" emotions send us messages something is not sound. Acknowledging why we experience distinct emotions assists you in

entrancing your target further. Anxiety's message is uncertainty. In the beginning times, we experienced anxiety and fear as an indicator of uncertainty. For our ancestors, uncertainty meant pain. Although we live in times where we don't need to worry precisely about physical danger (too much), we have different worries: emotional triggers. Avoiding pain is what motivates us.

Here are a few indicators of anxiety:

- Excessive laughter.
- Bathing in their own sweat.

HOW TO PSYCHOANALYZE SOMEONE

- Refraining from eye contact.
- Scattered eyes: looking everywhere.
- Disoriented focus.

How to discover what makes people anxious?

BRING UP A TOPIC THAT may serve as controversial, or a potential weakness. (See the section about insecurities.) Observe what topics invoke anxious behaviours. Then subtly talk about/around the subject.

Here's an example:

A GIRL WHO WE'LL CALL; Cherry lips. She displayed her anxiety through laughter.

She had the "me too syndrome" that was quite obvious. I stated an opinion. Her micro facial expressions expressed she disagreed. Her words were the opposite.

I tested the waters here. I asked her if she was seeing anyone. She told me no.

(I thought she may say yes). Anyway, I dismissed her. As soon as I indirectly dismissed her - she began laughing. (A symptom of her extreme anxiety).

I thought this was cute and wanted to see how far it could go. Since I had

discovered she has the "me too syndrome" I first voiced my controversial opinion and observed how she reacted. My opinion was that if you were to go with anyone,

they'd need to have money and a car. Women "like us" can't ruin our shoes.

She looked down - paused - laughed and hesitantly agreed. See - the ingredient to this would be increasing their anxiety. This is what differs between a person in a complacent relationship versus emotions running deep and wild. Stirring up these emotions create codependency.

What to do with this information:
NOTICE THEIR "NERVOUS" behaviors and pull it out of them. You'll begin to see what strikes their anxiety cords and you can play around with it.

Discover Their Fears

Maximizing pleasure and avoiding fear are how our personalities are born. Fear can haunt you for the rest of your life. As human beings - it is only natural to experience fear. It is one of our basic emotions. Our ancestors used fear for their survival, for example, fear of animals tearing them apart. Times have advanced, thus no need to worry about a threat towards our basic needs.

Why is this important?

The reason we still have fear? Fear protects us. Protection is not limited to our physical survival - but our emotional survival as well.

How to discover this?
FEARS CAN RANGE FROM spiders, to fingernails, to abandonment, to cheating. There are a few ways to discern what someone fears. It appears there are two types of fear. Fears like the "superficial" ones such as spiders. Deep rooted fears such as the fear of abandonment, and rejection are the second category of fear. Superficial fears go deeper than the surface and represent our deeper rooted fears. A fear of rats could potentially represent a fear of invasion or the lack of privacy in one's home. Watch for what they have an excessive amount of resistance to. An example of this would be someone who shows lots of resistance to someone who is considered wild. Reasons vary as to why someone would show an excessive amount of resistance to someone who is wild. Does this person remind them of someone who crushed their heart? Reminds them of their parents who abandoned them? Perhaps they desire someone to

show dedication and commitment, and a wild person reminds them they may not get that. Another thing to observe in a person is listen to the tone in their voice, do they avoid a specific topic? Does this topic have any kind of significance in their lives, specifically a negative one? Lastly, the most obvious one would be listen to what they say they are afraid of.

Example

THERE WAS A WOMAN WE will call Stephanie. From my analysis, I learned she had a fear of rejection as well as a fear of displeasing people. Using the fear then relief technique, I implied the idea that I may not want to be her friend anymore. There were several ways to go about this: the fastest way to do this is not speak to her. Truthfully I did not intentionally ignore Stephanie. My family has an annual traditional road trip. Unfortunately, texting outside my province was not included in my phone plan. Therefore, the only way to get a hold of me was via Whatsapp - which she did not have. She did have email but none of us had thought to use it. When I was back in town, my phone was blown up with an abundance of texts from Stephanie. "Are you okay - I haven't heard from you?", "Are you mad at me?". Texts along those lines in that order. The relief part comes in when I replied "Sorry *Steph** I forgot to tell you I was away!" She quickly replies "You should've told me! I was worried you were pissed off at me!" This validates my suspicions about her psyche, thus utilizing these techniques that induce fear, followed by relief.

How to use this information?

THERE ARE TWO WAYS to go about this information. Given this, you can use the fear followed by relief, or use pure fear to manipulate your target - or a mixture of both. Which techniques you use depend on your target.

Pure fear works on people who are the most secure. Examples include: people who feel existential boredom, or are very secure, someone who is too arrogant for their own good, weak minded, and someone who had to fight for what they wanted growing up.

Fear followed by relief work on people who have experienced traumatic experiences. Examples include thugs, soldiers, people growing up in unsafe homes. These types are seeking security. Provide security, but first provoke what they are familiar with - fear.

Prey on Your Target's Prominent Feeling State

What prominent emotions does your target experience the most?

Take any emotion that your target experiences often, and double it. For example, one of my past targets was always experiencing the longing and yearning. Amplify it. Be the only person who can provide these intense feelings.

Why is this important?

WE'RE INHERENTLY IN a feeling state. No matter what anyone says - we're more emotional than logical. Most of us (and I can bet) your target is reacting rather than responding. There is a difference. The difference is that reacting is emotional and responding is logical. Most of us, including myself - have a main feeling state. Sometimes they fluctuate, yet most of the time that emotional state stays the same.

Here's what I'm talking about:

LET'S PRETEND YOUR targets' feelings are superiority all day, everyday. You'll need to take those feelings and amplify it. This is because if their feelings are so intense, and you're the only person who can evoke those feelings - they'll become dependent on you. They won't even realize why they're becoming reliant on you.

How to discover their usual/favourite feelings are though?

WHAT ARE THEY CONSISTENTLY talking about? How do they say it? What memories come up in the conversation - examine the tone of that as well.

Example:

*LIAM'S FEELING STATE was nostalgia. I'd take him out and create memories. The next time I would see him I'd say: "omg - remember when we did X?" in a dreamy nostalgia state. His particular feeling state was the 80's. This was effortless for me - as I am watching 80's movies and listening to music from the 80's as well. I even dressed the part. My feelings of nostalgia rubbed off on him. (Remember: our mirror neurons - from "How to Make Someone Obsessed With You"). Other things I would do with Liam would be asking him about previous memories, anything of the past.

How did I know Liam's feeling state was nostalgia?

SIMPLE - THE 80'S WERE the only thing he ever spoke of. My observations were correct as he would come to me indulging in memories - something no one else would put up with.

What to do with this information:

LEARN WHAT THEIR FEELING state is - then aggravate it. You can provoke it by speaking around the topic, dressing the part, the tone in your voice, the look in your eye - get creative.

Chapter Seven

Personas They Wish To Be

WITH REGARDS TO MAKING someone obsessed with you, you must be able to detect which personas a person aspires to be. If you've read my first book, you would understand this would also be known as aggravating hidden sides they wish to explore, but feel unsafe to do so. Unfortunately this can backfire because their egos can start soaring. In the real world, people tend to confront you and/or call you out on your false pretenses. Telling others they are acting like something they aren't or shouldn't be, immediately creates resistance. On the other hand, maintain their delusions of who they affirm they are - and they're all yours.

Recurring Topics?

THE TOPICS THEY PERPETUALLY talk about indicates what identities/subcultures they've identified with and annexed themselves to. Matters they're always bringing up can denote their comfort zones, obnubilate personality traits, lastly - the archetype they long/trying to portray to the world.

How to take advantage of this:

It's easy to uncover what they're always bringing up. Just carefully listen - as most of the other chapters stress. Look beyond their words, and listen to how they say it, and their body language when they say it. It's that simple. You'll be able to detect concrete topics, people, and prevailing themes that represent archetypes and subcultures waiting to emerge.

SOME COMMON CONVERSATIONS *and their interpretations:*

"The other day I got so high and/or drunk with my friends". Or, they're always talking about their "little adventures with friends."

How to take advantage of this:

HOW TO PSYCHOANALYZE SOMEONE

They want to either be portrayed as someone who is popular and/or adventurous. Another meaning could be: hey, people acknowledge my existence and wish to be a component of it. I'm doing good fun things with my life - what are you doing with yours? Contribute to how astounding their lives are, and make them feel acknowledged.

Once in awhile you'll have to challenge them, and express things like "hey, thought you were adventurous - come on let's do this." Don't be insolent and verbalize things like "why aren't you doing anything on Friday? Thought you had a million friends?" That's rude and nonessential. Instead say " oh, you're conventionally up to something." Be classy about your ambiguity.

Another example:
"Everyone
does me wrong. I'm always so good to people but people do this to me".

How to take advantage of this:

This person is trying to portray the image of the victim and a potential drama queen. Both usually go hand in hand. Play the rescuer and allow them to be the victim by enabling their helplessness. Do not try to provide solutions like most people - sit there and listen quietly as they unload their idealizations of drama filled victim mentality.

Something else you can do, is wrong them. Give them a reason to drown in their martyr syndrome.

What to do with this information:

TO CONCLUDE, CAREFULLY discern what themes are extensive and allow your target to believe the image they are attempting to project has been projected onto you.

Chapter Eight

Their Expectations

EVERYONE HAS THEIR own expectations. In our own minds, we hold a series of expectations and if people don't fulfil them - we feel disappointed. This is the sole cause of disappointment; our expectations. In our heads, we have movies playing. Within these movies are roles people in our lives play, lines they must say to make the scene. If they don't - we feel angry behind the scenes if we are not self aware enough. The game of obsession is quite difficult to maintain as we must constantly adhere to our target's expectations. Failure to comply to their expectations may leave them feeling disappointed. However, when you succeed in complying to their expectations they so badly want fulfilled - expect them to be completely under your control. It is not common that everyday we come across people who are here to please us and us only. Take advantage of this, and understand their deepest expectations of what they would like from a person, and the world. Of course there are specific expectations where we do not have to comply. This chapter will show you how to discover what their expectations are.

Their "Love Language"

A conversation between two friends go something like this:
Friend A: I don't think my partner loves me.
Friend B: Why would you say that?
Friend A: He doesn't tell me he loves me.
Friend B: But he buys you flowers, and spends lots of time with you. I think he *does* love you.

What's happening here? The cliche conversation between the two friends is a perfect example of partners and people who don't understand their partner's love languages. The term is coined from the book "The Five Love Languages" by Dr. Gary Chapman. If you were an outsider listening in on the conversation, you might think the partner does indeed love her. However, friend A cannot see this because she has a subjective experience.

While I loved the book, Dr. Chapman never explained in full detail/analysis how to ascertain your target's love language - therefore I decided to add this part in the book.

Why is this important?

IN HER MIND, HER SIGNIFICANT other does not display love the way she *needs him to; verbally*. Friend A's partner may feel unappreciated, if she complained about him not "loving her", because in his mind - he is, via quality time/gifts. The lack of understanding of each partner's love language will create conflict within the relationship - even the death of it. Prevent conflict and create satisfaction by discovering your target's *love language*. As mentioned throughout this book: not one size fits all.

What are the five (5) love languages?

HOW TO PSYCHOANALYZE SOMEONE

GARY CHAPMAN DISCOVERED the five love languages which are:

- Quality Time
- Physical Touch
- Verbal Affirmation
- Gifts
- Acts of Service (which will not be explored here).

THE LOVE LANGUAGES are self explanatory. Thus I will not waste any time describing what all my readers already know. With each love language, I will explain three things:

1. How to detect this person has this love language.
2. How to appeal to their specific love language.
3. An example.

Quality Time
How you can tell:
They are always asking to do things with you.
Come up with some suggestions you can do for the weekend.
Shares things with you they've heard were fun and interesting.
Ensures you can spend more than just one hour with them.
Shares good times and memories, like that one time they got so wasted they stole a group of sick turtles.
An example:
Our egos have specific defense mechanisms. One of the mechanisms tends to be disliking something intensely if we know we cannot have it. A man who we'll call Bob, despised wealthy people. I discovered Bob grew up wealthy. Due to an unfortunate event, they lost their wealth. As a result of this, his mind chose to despise rich people as a way to cope with the loss of his family's wealth. Maybe this was a bit much, but for our

"quality time", I brought him to an elite bar where you need to actually hold elite status. My connections are of this circle, and they got me in.

I never told Bob of my connections. Despite this, he never questioned my "elite" status. We spent many hours at this bar. Slowly, but surely - he opened up about his childhood. The wealth. The poverty. Everything. Hell, I understood, my family went through a similar fate. As time went on, we scaled up to fancier bars. Throughout our time together, I recognized a belief: *rich people are evil.* Personally, I never believed this. There are evil people - affluent or poor. On the contrary, he was becoming what he "hated" the most. Taking him to these bars raised hell. Around me, he was experiencing cognitive dissonance. Bob went from calm and cool to aggressive, and money hungry. This is what was happening: Bob's ideal self and lifestyle was to return to his filthy rich life as a snotty spoiled young man. He resisted this idealization because in order to cope with the loss of wealth - his mind decided having a mediocre life made him a noble man.

He was riding a high up until the two of us could no longer afford to spend fuck you money at luxurious bars. He couldn't fulfil his needs, and I couldn't either. It was over. Given these circumstances - we fell apart. No more talks, or walks. Pure nothingness.

I enjoyed taking a break from the fast life. Spending thirty minutes putting on makeup to its highest level of perfection was no longer needed. Heels weren't required during my break, neither were the blisters that came with it. The slow life was the fun life. This was up until I was eager to experience some form of my former socialite life, so I picked up the phone and called my friend Luna. We went to this bar, and there was Bob. Sitting there with one of his buddies. He waved me over to have a seat with him and his friends. Fast forward into the night, Bob was completely out and his friend was the designated driver. He tells me he's heard lots about me, and that I've introduced Bob to this bar. He also went onto explain that Bob has been "different" since then. Bob's friend explained that they've known each other since they were children and that Bob now acts like that child he once knew. An important detail was shared here: Bob talked *a lot* about me, when he was drunk. Reminiscing in our memories, conversations detailing how we were going to rule the world. This one important detail showed me and now the readers of this book how important, better yet, love languages can be.

How to appeal to this:

Take the initiative, and do something that appeals to their personality. If you've discovered they're stuck in their head, take them out of their own minds by going to a place that will activate all their senses. They're an attention seeker? Bring your target to a place that will get them all the attention their heart desires.

PHYSICAL TOUCH

How you can tell:

A target who has this love language, is very touchy feely. Oftentimes they will speak about the texture of an item, or the feel of someone's skin. They are often the kinesthetic type. Listen to their words. Words such as: I *feel/felt/that feels so good/learns via hands on, rather than through theories.*

Example:

There was a girl whom we'll call Agnes. She was the perfect example of the physical touch. However, her need for touch varied. It was constantly fluctuating. One day when she was sad, she needed a hug. On a seperate day, she would appear distant. The solution was to allow her to lead. If she needed touch, I would provide that for her. Soon after, allowing her to lead, I soon discovered *why* she was distant, versus when she wanted physical affection. Many of her reasons had to do with *why* she was feeling despair. When she wanted affection in the form of physical touch, it was due to her feeling insecure about her worthiness. During times of displaying coldness, (where she didn't want physical affection, e.g. a hug) it was due to how some people would've treated her.

How to appeal to this:

Use touchy feely language. The words mentioned above are to be used - they are sufficient. As for actually physically touching them, you must discern the comfortability of their level of touching. If they are constantly in need of touch - accommodate. If you discover they want to be touched during specific times, during the need for security or affection, touch them during those times.

VERBAL AFFIRMATION

How you can tell:

They talk, almost brag about compliments they've received. They give you compliments. They're auditory. They're fantastic listeners, possibly good with the usage of words.

How to appeal to this and examples:

Easy. Give them compliments. Refer to this article I've written on *the art of smooth talking, originally written on November, 28th, 2015.*

So today I remembered the smooth talkers in my life. I don't have any more smooth talkers in my life. Because they piss me off. They piss me off because they don't understand HOW to smooth talk. The proper way. There is an art form. If you've done your homework on people now you'll fully understand this article.

Now, what is smooth talking? You usually hear of men being smooth talkers. They'll say anything to flatter a girl. A smooth talker is someone who has a way with words. Usually you can tell someone is a smooth talker by the way they talk. They're usually complimenting people. That's the most common sign.

If you want to be a proper smooth talker, you've got to understand what a person's weaknesses are. And their insecurities are. (Same shit.) But you also have to know what they're always being complimented on. Usually people have other people noticing and complimenting certain

HOW TO PSYCHOANALYZE SOMEONE 81

things on them. But most people desire to have someone notice, and compliment them on things they wish people could see.

Example:

In the categories of personas, I fit that incredibly beautiful out of everyone's league persona. So everyone always compliments me on being soo beautiful/sexy.

Or according to one guy I would be "the sexy beautiful crazy girl. Who is weird and totally oblivious to men hitting on her." I asked another friend and he says "yeah I can see that".

But if you were a smooth talker, you'd know their weaknesses. So for me, my weakness would be my intellect. I mean I know I'm intelligent. But, I'm kind of insecure about it. I'm also insecure about my ability to be able to make my future what I want it to be.

A smooth talker would compliment my intelligence. And how intelligent they think I am. But I hide my insecurities so well that no one would be able to tell I feel insecure about it. Unless we're close - you'd know.

Or, my ability to fit in with a regular crowd. I do horrible with crowds unless I know all of them. And I try to avoid crowds and hanging out with them like it's the plague. A smooth talker would tell me how much his friends or her friends loved me.

So the key is... finding out their hidden insecurities. Or things they wish people would notice.

Behind all that exterior is their core. So behind a preppy exterior is someone who wants to explore their crazy dark side. Behind a really hot girl or guy is someone who is more than just a pretty face... you get the point. (That's also where the phrase "opposites attract" come from.)

I felt this was the most important part of what we will call "smooth talking" because it's really the core of smooth talking. Knowing what appeals to them. The cords that'll strike their hearts. (Their hidden insecurities, their hidden selves yearning to come out.)

GIFTS

How you can tell:

They talk about gifts they've received, the best and worst, stores they love, what they're going to purchase next. Essentially, some of their conversations revolve around material items.

Example:

My style is quality time. Walks along the beach, delicious dinners. I befriended a lady who had the gift style. During the time I met her, she was in her late fifties. Although she acted like a child for her age, I was definitely attracted to her. She would take me out to dinner to lovely restaurants. That all changed when she lost money from an investment. I always knew she was the materialistic type, but saw this as my way to explore what kind of gifts she would need. From our conversations, she frequently discussed old memories of her youth when men admired her. She would then add that men still admired her. The perfect gift? Something that would accentuate her youth, and provoke desire within men. I was careful to make sure the gifts did not imply she was *withering and wrinkling like a prune in the sun*. These gifts included "brightening facial serum to bring out your inner glow", perfume, and other items of similar nature.

How to appeal to this:

Give your target gifts that satisfy their lacks, and emphasis the persona they want to show to the world.

I will not discuss "acts of services" as I cannot distinguish the difference between the two.

What to do with this information:

TRUTHFULLY, I'VE FOUND this to be very beneficial in my life. As you integrate this into your life, you will find that we all have our own "love languages" as Gary Chapman calls it. As you begin to play to people's love languages, you'll find that people will depend on you more.

Your Target's Deepest Fantasy: Make Them Come True.

Fantasies are a form of subconscious mind defence mechanism. There are many reasons why we develop fantasies as our preferred defence mechanism:

1. We, or your target was forced to stay inside as a child and watch tv. Especially cartoon and disney movies, causing the subconscious mind to utilize fantasies as a defense mechanism.

2. Your or their parents have always coerced them to be a certain way. Rather than playing different roles and giving the child the liberation to explore - their parents have placed restrictions on their child. Suppressing their desire to delve into different realities - thus engendering a child who turns to his/her fantasies to explore these fantasies.

3. Was raised in a very idealistic environment. Parents or guardians who use the words and/or phrases "that's unrealistic", "keep dreaming", "I'm just window shopping" ironically, raise children to become idealistic.

How would you discover your target's darkest fantasies?

Not only do you have to understand what their fantasies are, but you have to understand what kind of fantasies they are. The concrete types we have to understand are: idealized, suppressed, or unmet needs fantasies. Here is how to determine which fantasy is which.

Idealized selves:

This is their impeccable world - they are whoever they want to be, circumstances are precisely the way your target wants it. Fantasies insinuate an idealized self would be the tone in their voices - a dreamy tone that is. Your target may gravitate towards categorical movies, people, public figures.

Note that many people won't ever reveal what their fantasies are. Let alone have the self vigilance to analyze or categorize what their fantasies are.

Example:

A girl I knew was drawn to figures like Rihanna, watched tons of movies where girls were prostitutes, bad girl types. I know this is my persona as well. She secretly admired mean girl things I would do - such as: dismiss someone, or give someone an attitude on the street. I say secretly because she never overtly admitted - but there was a gleam in her eyes... Red in her cheeks - a curve on the ends of her mouth. In her waking life, she's a good girl. In her ideal world: she's liberated. She says what she wants when she wants - reveals some skin when desired and is a typical "bad girl".

Suppressed selves:

This is much like the idealized self except your target may or may not actually want to be this, because they're mainly afraid of these suppressed versions of themselves. An idealized self is someone they want to be. A suppressed self is someone who they could potentially want to be - but probably wouldn't. Not even in their deepest darkest fantasies. An example here would be a killer. A pedophile. A person who wants to become a prostitute. A violent person who shows everyone up. There may even be a hint of shame during these fantasies. Suppressed selves can stem from a curiosity of unacceptable social roles. You'll be able to tell this fantasy is a suppressed side through: People with specific suppressed sides are drawn to people who express their suppressed selves. The most common example is someone who plays with their dark sides draws noble people in. Rude people attract mild mannered persons. For more information, please see: what are they not?.

EXAMPLE:

I went on a trip to Asia. Prior to arriving in Asia, I was talking to a man who lives there. Ten minutes into meeting, I observed he was well coordinated, mindful, and lived in his head. We spoke for ten months prior to my arrival. Time and time again, I vowed I'd come to Asia. However, I was aware of his skepticism. Five months later - there I was. The man admitted he didn't believe I'd <u>actually</u> come to Asia. The conversation went like this:

Him: Wow, I'll admit I didn't think you'd actually come to Asia.

Me: I know. But when I say I'm going to do something - I'm going to do it.

Him: Wow, you're so wild. I wish I could be like that.

I hadn't realized how suppressed his adventurous side was until later that night I asked him if he would join me for a walk through an abandoned yard. "It's midnight." He says as he shoots me a puzzled/strange look.

My reply: "And, I'm only here for a few days. Let's go."

As we're going down the elevator he confesses he's never done something like this, but assumes I have. I'm casual about the entire thing because I do things like this often. Not only did I awaken his adventurous suppressed side, I allowed him to assume the lead. He planned how we'd break into the haunted area, and how we'd break out. He was much more adventurous than me, at that point. That was the objective - to allow his suppressed side to surface... To become one with his suppressed self. His body language loosened up. Enthusiasm consumed his being.

Not only was an adventurous side suppressed, but the desire to be "dirty." He seemed afraid of uncleanness. I allowed him to get his hands dirty - without any judgement. This would've been a night he's never forgotten.

Unmet need:

Unmet needs are needs that are not met. Your victim may speak in a tone that sounds like a mixture of longing and desperation.

Example:

Here's another vacation example when I went to Europe. Regarding European romances - I decided to go with the most cliche option: a Paris romance. Online, I began to chat with a French boy (I call him boy because he look and acted like one). Three years my junior. Things were casual - at first. Up until I began to say the things his heart and ego needed to hear for him to fall in love. He wasn't the best looking, but when I saw him on webcam - he was gorgeous. Observing from the look his face, he had no idea how attractive he looked - which made him much more appealing. Thirteen hours is how long we spoke everyday over Google hangouts. Several unmet needs revealed themselves:

- The need to feel attractive to the opposite sex, even praised, worshipped. How I could tell: easy - his wording. Once I asked little boy if he'd ever had a girlfriend. His answer was as expected: no. Abruptly he expressed that he had missed opportunities, and he was absolute on the fact that they had liked him. This wasn't it though - the part that revealed the need for praise was him sharing a story with me about a lass who displayed an interest in him. As the story progressed, his demeanor transitioned from kind gentleman to cocky teenage boy. He bragged about how much he had rejected her; how much she liked him.

- The need to be superior. His interests were primarily vulgar. Which explains his excessively nice demeanor - a coverup.

- Control. He questioned everything mainly with a "why", needed to hear reasons as to why I did what I did. The uncertainty drove him wild. He described his interaction with me as "climbing the world's tallest mountain".

You're expecting a paragraph about how I successfully fulfilled his needs? Unfortunately that's where I fail you. There was only one need I fulfilled so well, and it was the first one. The first one was enough to keep him obsessed but the next two needs were left unfulfilled. The way I left the two needs unmet were the worst ways I could leave them unmet: I gave him the opposite. The opposite was dangling my superiority and unpredictability in front of his big sparkly naive eyes. I went too far with dangling these things in front of him, I forgot I had to <u>actually</u> fulfill the next two needs. Occasionally I would, however there was not a balance between fulfilling and withdrawing his needs. As a result of this - fear lead him to running away. Poor little boy wouldn't even allow me to satisfy his sexual curiosity. Romantic and feelings of fear wouldn't allow him to go near me.

What to do with this information:

THE MOST IMPORTANT thing here is that how are you supposed to get them to express a fantasy. There are two ways you can go about this - possibly incorporating the two would be powerful. Watching a thought provoking movie. When the movie ends say "ya know..I've always had that type of fantasy." (I don't know - make some bullshit up) followed by; how about you? What do you fantasize about? Hint naughtiness in your voice. Not too naughty or they will tell you what their sexual fantasies are rather than an emotional fantasy they have. Imitating the conversation with a naughty secretive fantasy after a movie is perfect because you'd already get them into the flow. Everything just seemed so natural. It would seem that the movie has made you think of this rather than you strategically planned. When choosing a movie - make sure it's a dark movie.

If your target does not enjoy movies, tell them a story you heard about someone acting indecently attempting to satisfy a fantasy of theirs.

Some people walk around like dead zombies lacking any kind of imagination, or lacking the courage to explore their deepest, darkest fantasies. If revealing their fantasies is something you cannot easily hear from them, observe their behaviour. It is easy to understand which fantasies are which, and why they have particular fantasies they do.

Once you've gotten a good idea of what their fantasies may be - you must bring these fantasies to life. If you discover they fantasize about having people treat your target like a god - treat them like a God. If you understand they want to be romanced - romance them. You must know when to lead and when to allow them to lead.

Conclusion

Personality Profile

HOW TO PSYCHOANALYZE SOMEONE 89

NAME OF PERSON BEING profiled: "Dean"

The conclusion is what you've all been waiting for: a personal personality profile compiled together. You may notice broken sentences and notes. The reason being is, this is how you'll take notes on your target as well. When I was analyzing Dean, not every piece of information in each chapter applied to him. The information will be in order starting from chapter three. First, I'll state the information retrieved from my psychoanalysis, then actions to follow.

Chapter Three; Their past:
Relationship with parents; information:

- Disruptive.

- Mother dismissive, father physically abusive.

- Arguing about sex. Mother constantly wanted sex, felt unwanted. Father didn't want to have sex anymore because of lost libido. Mother esmasculated father. Therefore, possibly learned that saying yes to sex, even when not wanted - will make him a man.

Actions:

- Dismiss him.
- Display higher sex drive.
- Flaunt superior sexual past.
- Emasculate him.

FORMER FLAMES; INFORMATION:

- Physical exteriors of the women looked partially like prostitutes with substance abuse problems.

- Always came to the rescue.

- Allowed women to publicly humiliate him (emotionally).

Actions:

- Without looking like a prostitute with substance abuse issues, I seeked to have a look that may have represented what escorts with drug problems looked like. It was obvious Dean had slight misogynistic tendencies - just covered up with an extreme nice guy exterior. It's not his fault - look at who raised him. To closeted misogynists,escorts represent the lowest of the low. It's quite possible this is their chance to assert their perceived superiority over these women who need something from them: their money.

- I pursued my innocent looks, but had the attitude of a helpless young girl in need of another hit of her drug of choice. I had an advantage: my age. A girl my age could never have enough funds.. Or so he thought. I allowed for his tendanices to peek through. He finally felt control, he would give me money; I pretend to be his girlfriend in public. In private we were buddies who did coke together. He didn't even want to touch me.

Chapter Four; Their belief system:
What motivates them; information:

- Motivational words:

- "I have to"

- What motivates him is the avoidance of helplessness. Rather, his motivation was to feel as if he does finally have control.

Actions:

- When trying to motivate him, I made him feel he "had" to do things. There was a certain urgency. I would text him "Dean, we have to go to the movies. We're running out time!"

- When using what motivates him against him, I would imply certain actions could give him a feeling of control. When de-motivating Dean from committing an action, I expressed this action might make him feel powerless.

Chapter 5; defense mechanisms:
What are they not; information and actions:

- There are several forms of denial. Regarding Dean, he is trying to persuade someone he is something. In his case, it was that he was such a nice guy. Even an extreme feminist. I encouraged his act - but countered it by confessing I didn't understand why he "respected" women. Even going so far as to to expressing my "hatred" towards women. Slowly, his mysnoigist side came out... The side I waited for - to play with.

- Along with denial, he had defense mechanisms like undoing. He felt extreme guilt. This guilt was also used against him in very subtle ways.

Chapter 8; expectations:
Deepest fantasy; information:

- Suppressed: suppressed misogynist

Action:

- See defense mechanisms psychoanalysis and actions in this section.

- Ideal self:

- To be someone who is superior to women.

Action:

- Obtaining superiority above women can take on contrasting forms. Femininity is normally associated with being small, weak, sensitive. I displayed those traits in a very exaggerated manner. Calling him when I was emotional, breaking down at every "sad" part of the movie. He would tease me about "being such a girl". When I "broke down" he would command me to stop being such a girl. I did remind him I was a girl, and asked him what he meant by this. He smirked and replied "you're like a dude to me. So stop acting weak like a girl. This isn't you." My actions gave him the chance to finally experience his ideal self: superior to a woman who he perceived to be powerful (me).

- Unmet; psychoanalysis and action:

- Love from a woman. Unconditional love. Someone to make him feel like a man. Never received this. When I came around, I did provide the unconditional love... when I wasn't emasculating him.

HAVE FUN PSYCHOANALYZING your targets and getting into their heads - just remember not to lose yours.